The Success Mindset

Unlocking your Potential for Greatness

Copyright © 2023 by Anja Chambers.

All rights reserved.

No part of this book may be reproduced or transmitted in any form or by any means, electronic or mechanical, including photocopying, recording, or by any information storage and retrieval system, without permission in writing from the author.

This book was created with the assistance of an artificial intelligence program, and the author acknowledges the contributions of the program in the creation of this work. This book is for entertainment purposes only. The information and advice provided in this book are based on the author's personal experiences and opinions and should not be considered as professional or expert advice. The author and publisher are not liable for any damages or losses that may arise from the use of the information provided in this book. It is always recommended to seek professional advice and guidance before making any important decisions.

Finding Your Purpose 4

Overcoming Adversity 11

Developing Self-Awareness 18

Building Positive Habits 25

Pursuing Your Goals 32

Navigating Relationships 38

Cultivating Emotional Intelligence 45

Investing in Yourself 51

Taking Risks 59

Seeking and Accepting Help 64

Persevering Through Challenges 69

Maintaining Integrity and Values 75

Leaving a Legacy 80

Conclusion 86

Finding Your Purpose

The Importance of Knowing Your Why

Why do you get up in the morning? What drives you to keep going, even when things get tough? Knowing your why is the foundation for success in all areas of life. It gives you direction, motivation, and a sense of purpose. Without it, you may find yourself lost or unmotivated, lacking direction and fulfillment. In this chapter, we will explore the importance of knowing your why and how it can transform your life.

Defining Your Why

Your why is the reason you do what you do. It's the deep, underlying motivation behind your goals, actions, and decisions. It's not about what you do or how you do it, but rather why you do it. For some people, their why might be to help others, to make a difference in the world, to achieve financial freedom, or to create a fulfilling life. Your why should align with your values and beliefs and give you a sense of purpose and fulfillment.

Discovering Your Why

Discovering your why is not always easy. It requires introspection, self-reflection, and honesty with yourself. One way to start is by asking yourself a few questions:

- What brings me joy and fulfillment?
- What am I passionate about?
- What do I want to achieve in life?

- What legacy do I want to leave behind?

Another way to uncover your why is to look at the challenges and setbacks you've faced in your life. Often, these experiences can reveal important insights into your values and beliefs and what motivates you. For example, if you've experienced hardship and adversity, you may be driven by a desire to help others overcome similar challenges.

For me, discovering my why was a long and challenging journey. As a young adult, I struggled with anxiety and depression and felt lost and unmotivated. It wasn't until I started to explore my passions and interests that I began to uncover my why. I discovered that I was passionate about helping others and making a positive impact on the world.

Another personal example is the story of Simon Sinek, who is known for his work on the importance of knowing your why. Sinek had a successful career in advertising but felt unfulfilled and lacked direction. It wasn't until he discovered his why, which was to inspire others to do what inspires them, that he found true fulfillment and success. He has since become a bestselling author and speaker, inspiring countless individuals to discover their own why.

Transforming Your Life with Your Why

Knowing your why can transform your life in many ways. It gives you a sense of purpose and direction, motivating you to pursue your goals and dreams. It also helps you make decisions that align with your values and beliefs, leading to a more fulfilling and satisfying life. Additionally, your why can inspire and motivate others, creating a positive impact on the world.

In conclusion, discovering your why is a crucial step in winning in life. It gives you direction, motivation, and purpose, helping you achieve success and fulfillment in all areas of life. Take the time to explore your passions and values, and ask yourself what truly motivates and inspires you. Your why is waiting to be uncovered, and it can transform your life in ways you never thought possible.

Exploring Your Passions and Interests

Passion is the fuel that drives us to pursue our dreams and achieve greatness. It is the energy that keeps us going when the going gets tough. When you find your passion, you have found your purpose, and you can begin to create a life that is truly fulfilling. In this chapter, we will explore the importance of exploring your passions and interests and how it can help you find your purpose and win in life.

Discovering Your Passions and Interests

Exploring your passions and interests is a vital step in finding your purpose. When you do things that you love, you feel alive, energized, and fulfilled. However, many people struggle to identify their passions and interests, especially if they have spent most of their lives doing things that they don't enjoy. Here are some tips to help you discover your passions and interests:

1. Pay Attention to What Makes You Happy: What activities do you enjoy doing in your free time? What makes you lose track of time and feel fully engaged in the moment? These activities can be clues to your passions and interests.

2. Think Back to Your Childhood: What did you love to do as a child? Often, the things we loved to do as children are still relevant to our passions and interests as adults.
3. Try New Things: Don't be afraid to try new activities or hobbies. You may discover a new passion that you never knew existed.

For me, exploring my passions and interests was a long and winding journey. As a child, I loved to read and write, but I never considered pursuing these interests as a career. Instead, I followed a more conventional path and pursued a degree in business. However, after working in the corporate world for several years, I realized that I wasn't happy and felt unfulfilled. It wasn't until I started to explore my passions and interests that I found my true purpose. I began to write in my free time and eventually started a blog. Writing became my passion, and I decided to pursue it as a full-time career. Today, I am a writer, and I feel fulfilled and happy doing what I love.

Another personal example is the story of J.K. Rowling, the author of the Harry Potter series. Before she wrote the series, Rowling was a struggling single mother living on welfare. However, she had always been passionate about writing, and she used her love of storytelling to create the magical world of Harry Potter. Today, she is one of the most successful authors of all time, and her books have sold over 500 million copies worldwide.

Following Your Passion

Once you have discovered your passion, it's important to take action to pursue it. This can be a scary step, especially if your passion doesn't align with your current career or lifestyle. However, following your passion is essential to finding true fulfillment and happiness in life. Here are some tips for following your passion:

1. Make a Plan: Create a plan to pursue your passion, whether it's taking a class, starting a side hustle, or going back to school.
2. Take Small Steps: Don't feel like you have to make a huge leap to pursue your passion. Start small and take baby steps to build momentum.
3. Be Persistent: Pursuing your passion can be challenging, and setbacks are inevitable. However, if you stay persistent and keep moving forward, you can achieve your goals.

In conclusion, exploring your passions and interests is a vital step in finding your purpose and winning in life. When you do things that you love, you feel alive, energized, and fulfilled. Take the time to discover your passions and interests and take action to pursue them. You never know where they may

Defining Success for Yourself

Success means different things to different people. For some, success is measured by material possessions, while for others, it's about achieving personal goals or making a positive impact on the world. However, in order to truly win in life, it's important to define success for yourself. In this subchapter, we will explore the importance of defining success for yourself and how it can help you achieve your goals and live a fulfilling life.

Why Define Success for Yourself

Defining success for yourself is important because it allows you to create a life that is aligned with your values, passions, and purpose. When you define success based on external factors such as societal norms or other people's expectations, you may achieve those goals, but you may not feel fulfilled or happy. By defining success for yourself, you can create a life that is true to who you are and what you want to achieve.

Defining Success for Yourself

When defining success for yourself, it's important to consider the following:

1. Your Values: What are the things that are most important to you? Your values may include things like honesty, integrity, family, and community.
2. Your Passions: What are the things that you love to do? Your passions may include things like writing, art, music, or sports.
3. Your Purpose: What is the impact that you want to make on the world? Your purpose may be to make a positive difference in the lives of others, to create a better world, or to inspire others to pursue their dreams.

For me, defining success for myself has been a journey of self-discovery. Growing up, I was always taught that success meant achieving good grades, getting a good job, and earning a lot of money. However, as I got older, I realized that these external factors didn't bring me true fulfillment and happiness. It wasn't until I took the time to define success for myself that I found my purpose and began to live a more fulfilling life. Today, I define success based on my values of honesty, integrity, and making a positive impact on the world. I feel fulfilled and happy pursuing my passions and using my skills to help others.

Another personal example is the story of Oprah Winfrey. Oprah grew up in poverty and faced many challenges in her life. However, she defined success for herself as making a positive impact on the world and empowering others to do the same. Today, she is one of the most successful media moguls in the world, and she has used her platform to make a positive difference in the lives of millions of people.

Living a Successful Life

Once you have defined success for yourself, it's important to take action to achieve your goals. Here are some tips for living a successful life:

1. Set Goals: Set goals that are aligned with your values, passions, and purpose.
2. Take Action: Take action towards your goals every day, no matter how small.
3. Celebrate Your Wins: Celebrate your successes, no matter how small, and use them as motivation to keep moving forward.

In conclusion, defining success for yourself is an essential step in winning in life. When you define success based on your values, passions, and purpose, you can create a life that is fulfilling and aligned with who you are. Take the time to define success for yourself, set goals, and take action towards achieving them. You have the power to create a successful life on your own terms.

Overcoming Adversity

Understanding the Nature of Adversity

Adversity is a part of life that we all face at some point. Whether it's a personal setback or a global crisis, adversity can be challenging and difficult to navigate. In this chapter, we will explore the nature of adversity, why it's important to understand it, and how we can overcome it to achieve our goals and live a fulfilling life.

The Nature of Adversity

Adversity can come in many forms, including:

1. Personal setbacks: These can include things like illness, injury, financial hardship, or the loss of a loved one.
2. Professional challenges: These can include things like job loss, career setbacks, or difficulty finding work.
3. Global crises: These can include things like natural disasters, pandemics, or political unrest.

Regardless of the form it takes, adversity can be difficult to face. It can leave us feeling overwhelmed, anxious, and unsure of how to move forward.

Why Understanding Adversity is Important

Understanding the nature of adversity is important because it can help us navigate challenging situations more effectively. When we understand that adversity is a natural part of life, we can approach it with a more positive mindset and develop the resilience needed to overcome it. By understanding that adversity is not something that we can always control, we can focus on the things that we can control, such as our response to the situation.

Overcoming Adversity

Overcoming adversity requires a combination of resilience, perseverance, and a positive mindset. Here are some tips for overcoming adversity:

1. Develop Resilience: Resilience is the ability to bounce back from setbacks and challenges. It can be developed through mindfulness practices, building supportive relationships, and reframing negative thoughts into positive ones.
2. Set Realistic Goals: Setting goals that are achievable can help build confidence and motivation, even during difficult times.
3. Practice Self-Care: Taking care of your physical, emotional, and mental health can help you build the strength and resilience needed to overcome adversity.

Adversity has played a significant role in my own life. When I was in college, I faced a serious health challenge that required multiple surgeries and months of recovery time. During this time, I felt overwhelmed and unsure of how to move forward. However, by focusing on building resilience, setting realistic goals, and practicing self-care, I was able to overcome this challenge and graduate with honors.

Another personal example is the story of J.K. Rowling, the author of the Harry Potter series. Before she became a successful author, Rowling faced many challenges, including poverty, depression, and rejection. However, through perseverance and a positive mindset, she was able to overcome these challenges and become one of the most successful authors of all time.

In conclusion, understanding the nature of adversity is an important step in overcoming it. By developing resilience, setting realistic goals, and practicing self-care, we can navigate challenging situations more effectively and achieve our goals. Remember that adversity is a natural part of life, and that by focusing on the things that we can control, we can overcome even the most difficult challenges.

Cultivating Resilience and Grit

Resilience and grit are two essential traits that can help us overcome adversity and achieve success. In this chapter, we will explore what resilience and grit are, why they are important, and how we can cultivate these traits to achieve our goals and live a fulfilling life.

What is Resilience?

Resilience is the ability to bounce back from setbacks and challenges. It is the mental toughness and emotional strength that allows us to overcome adversity and continue moving forward. Resilience is not something that we are born with; it is something that we can develop and cultivate through practice.

What is Grit?

Grit is a term coined by psychologist Angela Duckworth, which refers to the combination of passion and perseverance needed to achieve long-term goals. Grit is about staying committed to a goal, even in the face of challenges and setbacks. Like resilience, grit is a trait that can be developed and cultivated over time.

Why are Resilience and Grit Important?

Resilience and grit are important because they help us overcome adversity and achieve our goals. They allow us to stay motivated, focused, and committed, even when things get tough. Resilience and grit are also important because they help us build confidence and self-efficacy, which can lead to greater success in all areas of life.

Cultivating Resilience and Grit

Here are some ways to cultivate resilience and grit:

1. Practice Mindfulness: Mindfulness is a practice that can help us stay present and focused, even during difficult times. Mindfulness can help us build resilience by allowing us to stay calm and centered in the face of adversity.
2. Embrace Failure: Failure is a natural part of the learning process. Embracing failure and seeing it as an opportunity to learn and grow can help us build resilience and grit.
3. Develop a Growth Mindset: A growth mindset is the belief that we can develop our abilities through hard work and dedication. Developing a growth

mindset can help us stay committed to our goals, even when faced with challenges and setbacks.
4. Seek Support: Building supportive relationships with friends, family, and mentors can help us build resilience and grit. Supportive relationships can provide encouragement, advice, and a listening ear when we need it most.

Growing up, I faced a number of challenges that required me to develop resilience and grit. One of the biggest challenges was when my parents divorced. This was a difficult time for me, but I learned to stay focused on my goals and to rely on the support of my family and friends. By cultivating resilience and grit, I was able to graduate from college with honors and pursue a successful career in my field.

Another personal example is the story of Michael Jordan. Jordan was cut from his high school basketball team, but he used this setback as motivation to work harder and develop his skills. Through perseverance and a commitment to his goals, Jordan went on to become one of the greatest basketball players of all time.

In conclusion, resilience and grit are essential traits that can help us overcome adversity and achieve our goals. By practicing mindfulness, embracing failure, developing a growth mindset, and seeking support, we can cultivate these traits and live a more fulfilling life. Remember that resilience and grit are not something that we are born with, but rather something that we can develop and cultivate through practice.

Finding Opportunity in Setbacks

Setbacks are a natural part of life, and they can be frustrating and discouraging. However, setbacks can also present opportunities for growth and development. In this subchapter, we will explore how to find opportunity in setbacks and turn adversity into advantage.

Reframe Your Thinking

The first step to finding opportunity in setbacks is to reframe your thinking. Instead of seeing setbacks as failures, see them as opportunities to learn and grow. Ask yourself: what can I learn from this experience? What skills can I develop as a result of this setback? How can I use this experience to become a better person?

Embrace Change

Setbacks often require us to make changes in our lives. Embrace these changes and see them as opportunities to try new things and explore new opportunities. Remember that change can be uncomfortable, but it can also lead to growth and new experiences.

Take Action

Once you have reframed your thinking and embraced change, it's time to take action. Identify the steps you need to take to overcome the setback and achieve your goals. Remember that small steps can lead to big results, so focus on taking consistent action, even if it's just one step at a time.

One personal example of finding opportunity in setbacks comes from my own life. A few years ago, I was laid off from my job due to company downsizing. At first, I felt discouraged and uncertain about my future. However, I decided to use this setback as an opportunity to explore new career paths and learn new skills. I started taking courses in digital marketing and social media management and eventually landed a job in a new field that I love.

Another example is the story of J.K. Rowling, who faced numerous setbacks and rejections before becoming a best-selling author. Despite these setbacks, Rowling never gave up on her dream of becoming a writer. She continued to work on her craft and eventually landed a publishing deal for the first Harry Potter book. Today, she is one of the most successful authors of all time.

In conclusion, setbacks can be frustrating and discouraging, but they can also present opportunities for growth and development. By reframing your thinking, embracing change, and taking action, you can turn adversity into advantage and achieve your goals. Remember that setbacks are a natural part of life, and they can be overcome with persistence, resilience, and a positive attitude.

Developing Self-Awareness

Recognizing Your Strengths and Weaknesses

In order to succeed in life, it's important to have a clear understanding of your strengths and weaknesses. By recognizing what you're good at and where you need improvement, you can make better decisions, set more realistic goals, and achieve greater success.

Identify Your Strengths

Your strengths are the things you do well and enjoy doing. They are the skills and qualities that make you stand out from others. Identifying your strengths is essential to achieving success, because it allows you to focus on the things that you're good at and build upon them.

To identify your strengths, start by reflecting on your past accomplishments. What have you done well in the past? What do others compliment you on? What activities do you enjoy doing? Ask friends, family, and coworkers for their feedback, as they may see strengths in you that you don't see in yourself.

Identify Your Weaknesses

Your weaknesses are the areas where you need improvement. They are the skills and qualities that you struggle with and may hold you back from achieving your goals. Identifying your weaknesses is important because it allows you to address them and work on improving them.

To identify your weaknesses, start by reflecting on your past experiences where you struggled or received negative feedback. What areas do you feel you need improvement in? What skills do you lack? Be honest with yourself, but also recognize that everyone has weaknesses and it's okay to need improvement.

One personal example of recognizing my strengths and weaknesses comes from my experience in public speaking. In high school, I was terrified of public speaking and would avoid it at all costs. However, in college, I realized that public speaking was an important skill to have and decided to face my fear. I joined a public speaking club and received feedback from others on my strengths and weaknesses. Through this process, I discovered that I was good at storytelling and connecting with the audience, but struggled with maintaining eye contact and using vocal variety. Knowing this, I was able to focus on improving these areas and eventually became much more confident in my public speaking abilities.

Another example is the story of Michael Jordan, who is widely considered one of the greatest basketball players of all time. Despite his natural talent, Jordan recognized his weaknesses and worked tirelessly to improve them. He practiced relentlessly, worked on his conditioning, and improved his jump shot, eventually becoming an unstoppable force on the court.

In conclusion, recognizing your strengths and weaknesses is essential to achieving success. By identifying your strengths, you can focus on what you're good at and build upon it. By identifying your weaknesses, you can address them and work on improving them. Remember that everyone has strengths and weaknesses, and it's okay to need improvement. By embracing your strengths and working on your weaknesses, you can achieve greater success and fulfillment in life.

Identifying Your Values and Beliefs

Your values and beliefs are the guiding principles that shape your behavior and decisions in life. They are deeply personal and can have a significant impact on your happiness and fulfillment. Identifying your values and beliefs is important because it helps you understand what truly matters to you and can guide you towards making choices that align with your authentic self.

Identifying Your Values

Values are the things that are most important to you in life. They can include things like honesty, integrity, family, spirituality, success, or adventure. Identifying your values helps you understand what motivates and inspires you, and can help guide you towards making choices that are in alignment with your priorities.

To identify your values, start by reflecting on the times in your life when you felt most fulfilled and satisfied. What was it about those experiences that made them meaningful to you? What core principles or values were present in those moments? Consider also what you would be willing to fight for or sacrifice for. Your values will be unique to you, and there are no right or wrong answers.

Identifying Your Beliefs

Beliefs are the assumptions and convictions that you hold about yourself, others, and the world around you. They can include things like beliefs about your abilities, the nature of the world, and the roles that others play in your life. Your beliefs can be empowering or limiting, depending on how they serve you.

To identify your beliefs, start by reflecting on the messages that you have received throughout your life from family, friends, society, and culture. Consider how these messages have influenced your self-perception and worldview. Pay attention to your self-talk and the stories that you tell yourself about your abilities and potential. Challenge any limiting beliefs that may be holding you back from achieving your goals.

One example of identifying your values and beliefs the story of Malala Yousafzai, a young woman from Pakistan who became an advocate for education and women's rights after surviving an assassination attempt by the Taliban. Malala's values of education and equality were deeply ingrained in her from a young age, and her beliefs about the power of education and the importance of standing up for what is right guided her towards becoming an international advocate for these issues.

In conclusion, identifying your values and beliefs is an important step towards living a fulfilling and authentic life. By understanding what truly matters to you and what beliefs may be limiting you, you can make choices that align with your priorities and work towards achieving your goals. Remember that your values and beliefs are unique to you, and it's okay to challenge beliefs that no longer serve you or align with your priorities. By staying true to yourself and living in alignment with your values and beliefs, you can achieve greater happiness and fulfillment in life.

Practicing Mindfulness and Reflection

In today's fast-paced and busy world, it's easy to get caught up in the rush of daily life and lose sight of our goals and values. Practicing mindfulness and reflection can help us slow down and reconnect with ourselves, leading to greater clarity, focus, and fulfillment.

What is Mindfulness?

Mindfulness is the practice of paying attention to the present moment without judgment. It involves bringing our awareness to our thoughts, feelings, and sensations in the moment, rather than getting caught up in worries about the future or regrets about the past. Practicing mindfulness can help reduce stress, improve focus and concentration, and increase overall well-being.

One way to practice mindfulness is through meditation. This involves finding a quiet and comfortable space, sitting with your eyes closed, and focusing your attention on your breath or a specific object. When your mind wanders, simply notice the distraction and gently bring your attention back to your breath or object.

Another way to practice mindfulness is through everyday activities, such as eating, walking, or even brushing your teeth. Simply focus your attention on the sensations of the activity, rather than letting your mind wander to other thoughts or worries.

What is Reflection?

Reflection is the process of looking back on our experiences and examining them with curiosity and openness. It involves asking ourselves questions like "What did I learn from this experience?" or "What could I have done differently?" Reflection can help us gain insight into ourselves, our values, and our priorities, and can guide us towards making more intentional choices in the future.

One way to practice reflection is through journaling. Set aside time each day or week to write down your thoughts and feelings about your experiences. Ask yourself questions like "What am I grateful for today?" or "What challenges did I face this week and how did I handle them?" Reflecting on your experiences in writing can help you gain clarity and perspective, and can serve as a tool for tracking your progress towards your goals.

One personal example of practicing mindfulness and reflection came during a period of high stress in my life. I was juggling a demanding job, caring for my young children, and managing a household, and often felt overwhelmed and exhausted. By incorporating daily meditation and mindfulness practices into my routine, I was able to better manage my stress and find moments of calm amidst the chaos.

Another example came when I was struggling with a difficult decision. I took time to reflect on my values and priorities, and wrote down my thoughts and feelings about the situation in a journal. Through this process, I was able to gain clarity about what was most important to me, and was able to make a decision that aligned with my values and goals.

In conclusion, practicing mindfulness and reflection are powerful tools for reconnecting with ourselves and living more intentional and fulfilling lives. By slowing down and paying attention to the present moment, we can reduce stress and increase well-being. By reflecting on our experiences and examining them with curiosity and openness, we can gain insight into ourselves and our values, and can make choices that align with our authentic selves.

Building Positive Habits

The Power of Habits in Success

Habits are the building blocks of success. The things we do consistently day in and day out shape our lives and determine our outcomes. Developing good habits and breaking bad ones is key to achieving our goals and living the life we want.

What are Habits?

Habits are behaviors that we perform automatically, without much thought or effort. They are often formed through repetition, and become ingrained in our brains and bodies over time. Habits can be good or bad, and can have a profound impact on our lives.

The Power of Good Habits

Developing good habits is essential for success. Good habits can help us achieve our goals, improve our health and well-being, and increase our productivity and effectiveness. Examples of good habits include exercising regularly, eating healthy foods, practicing gratitude, and setting aside time for self-care and personal development.

One way to develop good habits is through the process of habit stacking. This involves linking a new habit to an existing one, so that the existing habit serves as a trigger for the new one. For example, if you want to start meditating every morning, you could link it to the habit of making coffee. Every morning, after you make your coffee, you could sit down and meditate for a few minutes. Over time, this habit stack becomes automatic, and you will start to reap the benefits of a regular meditation practice.

The Challenge of Breaking Bad Habits

Breaking bad habits is often much more challenging than developing good ones. Bad habits are often deeply ingrained, and can be difficult to recognize and change. Examples of bad habits include procrastination, negative self-talk, and unhealthy coping mechanisms like drinking or smoking.

One way to break bad habits is to identify the trigger that leads to the behavior, and then replace the behavior with a more positive one. For example, if you tend to reach for a cigarette when you feel stressed, you could replace that behavior with a walk outside or deep breathing exercises.

One personal example of the power of habits came when I decided to start exercising regularly. I began by setting a goal to work out for just 10 minutes a day, every day. Over time, that habit grew into a regular exercise routine that I looked forward to each day. This habit not only improved my physical health, but also my mental and emotional well-being.

Another personal example came when I realized that I had developed a bad habit of negative self-talk. I began to pay attention to my inner dialogue, and made a conscious effort to replace negative thoughts with more positive ones. This habit shift had a profound impact on my self-esteem and confidence, and helped me achieve my goals with more ease and joy.

In conclusion, the power of habits cannot be underestimated in the pursuit of success. Developing good habits and breaking bad ones takes time and effort, but the payoff is worth it. By focusing on building habits that align with our goals and values, we can create the life we want and achieve success on our own terms.

Strategies for Creating and Maintaining Good Habits

Creating and maintaining good habits is key to achieving success in life. Habits are actions that we perform on a daily basis, often unconsciously. They are formed through repetition and become automatic, making them a powerful force in our lives. Developing good habits is important because they can help us achieve our goals and make positive changes in our lives. In this section, we will discuss strategies for creating and maintaining good habits.

1. Start small: One of the most effective ways to create a new habit is to start small. Choose one habit you want to develop and focus on that. For example, if you want to start exercising, begin with a short workout routine or a daily walk. Once that habit is established, you can gradually increase the time and intensity.
2. Set goals: Setting goals can help you stay motivated and focused on creating good habits. Make sure your goals are specific, measurable, and achievable. For example, if you want to read more, set a goal to read for 30 minutes each day.
3. Create a routine: Habits are formed through repetition, so creating a routine can be helpful in establishing a new habit. Set a specific time and

place for your habit, and stick to it as much as possible. For example, if you want to start meditating, create a routine where you meditate for 10 minutes each morning.
4. Stay accountable: Find someone who can help keep you accountable for your new habit. This can be a friend, family member, or even a coach. Having someone who is aware of your goal and progress can help keep you motivated and on track.
5. Track your progress: Keep track of your progress in developing your new habit. This can be as simple as crossing off days on a calendar or using an app that tracks your progress. Seeing your progress can be a great motivator and help you stay committed to your new habit.
6. Reward yourself: Reward yourself for reaching milestones in your new habit development. This can be a small treat, like a favorite snack or a movie, or something bigger like a weekend getaway. Rewarding yourself can help reinforce the positive behavior and make it easier to continue.
7. Don't give up: Remember that creating a new habit takes time and effort. It's easy to become discouraged if you slip up or miss a day, but don't give up. Use setbacks as an opportunity to learn and improve, and keep pushing forward.

Developing good habits is a lifelong process, but it can be a rewarding one. The key is to start small, set goals, create a routine, stay accountable, track your progress, reward yourself, and never give up. By following these strategies, you can create and maintain good habits that will help you achieve success in life.

Breaking Bad Habits and Overcoming Temptation

Breaking bad habits and overcoming temptation is essential for achieving success. Bad habits can derail our progress and leave us feeling unfulfilled and disappointed. However, breaking these habits can be a challenging process. This subchapter will explore strategies for identifying and breaking bad habits, as well as overcoming temptation.

Identifying Bad Habits

The first step in breaking bad habits is to identify them. Bad habits are behaviors that are detrimental to our well-being, goals, and success. Some common bad habits include procrastination, overeating, overspending, smoking, and excessive social media use.

To identify your bad habits, start by reflecting on your daily routine and behaviors. Ask yourself what behaviors are holding you back from achieving your goals. You may also want to ask friends or family members for feedback on areas where they think you could improve.

Strategies for Breaking Bad Habits

Once you have identified your bad habits, it's time to start breaking them. Here are some strategies for breaking bad habits:

1. Start Small: Trying to change too many habits at once can be overwhelming. Instead, focus on one habit at a time. Start with something small, such as reducing your social media use by 30 minutes per day.

2. Find a Replacement: Often, bad habits serve a purpose in our lives, such as reducing stress or providing comfort. To break the habit, find a replacement behavior that serves the same purpose. For example, if you smoke to reduce stress, try going for a walk or practicing meditation instead.
3. Create Accountability: Share your goals with others and ask them to hold you accountable. Having someone to report to can help keep you motivated and on track.
4. Reward Yourself: Celebrate your successes along the way. Reward yourself for breaking a bad habit by treating yourself to something you enjoy, such as a favorite meal or activity.

Overcoming Temptation

Breaking bad habits requires willpower and determination. However, even the strongest willpower can falter when faced with temptation. Here are some strategies for overcoming temptation:

1. Avoid Triggers: Identify situations or environments that trigger your bad habit and avoid them. For example, if you tend to overeat when watching TV, try reading a book instead.
2. Change Your Environment: Make changes to your environment that support your goals. For example, if you want to reduce your alcohol consumption, remove alcohol from your home.
3. Practice Self-Care: Taking care of yourself can help reduce stress and increase willpower. Get enough sleep, eat a healthy diet, and exercise regularly.

4. Visualize Success: Imagine yourself succeeding in breaking your bad habit. Visualize the benefits of breaking the habit and how it will improve your life.

In conclusion, breaking bad habits and overcoming temptation is critical for achieving success. By identifying bad habits, using strategies to break them, and overcoming temptation, we can develop better habits and move closer to our goals.

Pursuing Your Goals

Setting SMART Goals

Goals are an essential part of any successful person's journey. Without a clear understanding of what you want to achieve, it can be challenging to make progress towards your desired outcome. Setting goals helps you to focus your attention and energy on specific areas of your life, enabling you to achieve more significant success in less time.

However, not all goals are created equal. Setting vague, unrealistic, or unattainable goals can leave you feeling frustrated, unmotivated, and disheartened. That's why it's essential to set SMART goals, a framework designed to help you create objectives that are specific, measurable, achievable, relevant, and time-bound.

Here's how each of the SMART goal criteria can help you create effective goals:

1. Specific: Clearly define what you want to achieve. The more specific your goal, the more likely you are to achieve it. Vague goals like "I want to be successful" won't give you a clear direction to follow.

Example: I want to improve my public speaking skills so that I can deliver a TED talk by the end of the year.

2. Measurable: Establish how you will measure your progress towards your goal. Defining concrete

criteria for measuring progress helps you stay motivated and focused.

Example: I will measure my progress by delivering at least one public speech every month, gradually increasing the length of each speech, and receiving positive feedback from my audience.

3. Achievable: Make sure your goal is realistic and attainable. Setting an impossible goal will leave you feeling overwhelmed and frustrated.

Example: Based on my current public speaking skills and available resources, I will set aside time every day to practice my speeches and attend workshops to improve my skills.

4. Relevant: Ensure that your goal is relevant to your overall life vision and mission. Having a clear understanding of your core values and beliefs can help you set goals that align with your aspirations.

Example: Improving my public speaking skills will help me become a more effective communicator, which is essential to achieving my ultimate goal of becoming a thought leader in my industry.

5. Time-bound: Set a deadline for achieving your goal. A timeframe creates a sense of urgency and helps you stay focused and motivated.

Example: I will deliver my TED talk by December 31st, giving me nine months to achieve my goal.

In conclusion, setting SMART goals is a powerful tool for achieving success. It helps you create specific, measurable, achievable, relevant, and time-bound objectives, making it easier to focus your energy and attention. By following the SMART framework, you can set yourself up for success and achieve your desired outcome.

Creating a Plan of Action

After setting SMART goals, the next step is to create a plan of action that will help you achieve those goals. A plan of action involves breaking down your goals into smaller, actionable steps and creating a timeline for each step. This ensures that you stay on track and make progress towards your goals.

Here are some tips for creating a plan of action:

1. Break down your goals: Break your larger goals into smaller, more manageable steps. This makes it easier to focus on each step and track your progress. For example, if your goal is to write a book, break it down into smaller steps like creating an outline, writing the first chapter, and so on.
2. Set deadlines: Set a deadline for each step of your plan. This gives you a clear timeline to work towards and ensures that you make progress towards your goal.
3. Prioritize your tasks: Prioritize the tasks in your plan based on their importance and urgency. This helps you focus on the most important tasks first and ensures that you use your time effectively.

4. Stay flexible: Be open to making changes to your plan as needed. Life can be unpredictable, and sometimes unexpected events may occur that require you to adjust your plan.
5. Track your progress: Keep track of your progress towards each step of your plan. This helps you stay motivated and gives you a sense of accomplishment as you complete each step.

When I set a goal to improve my fitness level, I created a plan of action that involved breaking down my goal into smaller steps like going for a daily walk, joining a gym, and tracking my progress. I set deadlines for each step and prioritized my tasks based on their importance. As I progressed through my plan, I tracked my progress and made adjustments as needed. This helped me stay motivated and focused on my goal, and I was able to achieve my desired fitness level.

Staying Motivated and Focused

Staying motivated and focused is a critical aspect of achieving success in life. When we first start on a new project or goal, we are usually full of enthusiasm and motivation. However, as time goes on, our motivation can wane, and we may struggle to stay focused on our goals. In this subchapter, we will discuss some strategies for staying motivated and focused, even when things get tough.

1. Develop a Strong "Why": As we discussed in an earlier subchapter, knowing your "why" is essential for success. When you have a strong reason for pursuing your goals, it can help you stay motivated

and focused, even during challenging times. Take some time to reflect on your "why" and write it down. Keep your "why" somewhere you can see it regularly, such as on a vision board or in a journal.
2. Break Down Your Goals: Sometimes, when we set large, lofty goals, they can feel overwhelming. This feeling of overwhelm can lead to a lack of motivation and focus. One way to combat this is by breaking down your goals into smaller, more manageable steps. This will help you see progress along the way and give you a sense of accomplishment that can help you stay motivated.
3. Celebrate Small Wins: Celebrating your successes, no matter how small, can be a powerful motivator. When you achieve a small goal or make progress towards a larger one, take the time to acknowledge it and celebrate it. This could be as simple as taking a few minutes to reflect on your accomplishment or treating yourself to something you enjoy.
4. Surround Yourself with Supportive People: Surrounding yourself with people who support and encourage you can be a powerful motivator. Seek out friends, family members, or colleagues who believe in you and your goals. You can also join groups or communities of like-minded individuals who share your values and aspirations.
5. Visualize Your Success: Visualization is a powerful tool for staying motivated and focused. Take some time each day to visualize yourself achieving your goals. Imagine what it will feel like to accomplish your dreams and how it will positively impact your life.
6. Stay Accountable: Having someone to hold you accountable can help you stay motivated and focused. This could be a friend, family member, or

even a coach. Share your goals with someone you trust and ask them to check in with you regularly to see how you're doing.
7. Take Care of Yourself: Finally, taking care of your physical and emotional well-being is essential for staying motivated and focused. Make sure you're getting enough rest, eating well, and engaging in activities that bring you joy and fulfillment. When you feel good physically and emotionally, it can be easier to stay motivated and focused on your goals.

Personal Example:

When I was working on my master's degree, there were times when I felt overwhelmed and unmotivated. One of the strategies that helped me stay focused was breaking down my goals into smaller, more manageable steps. I created a schedule for myself that included regular study sessions and breaks, and I made sure to celebrate my small wins along the way. I also surrounded myself with supportive friends and family members who encouraged me and reminded me of my "why." Additionally, I made sure to take care of myself by getting enough sleep, eating well, and engaging in regular exercise. All of these strategies helped me stay motivated and focused, and I ultimately achieved my goal of earning my master's degree.

Navigating Relationships

The Importance of Healthy Relationships

When it comes to achieving success in life, the importance of healthy relationships cannot be overstated. Our relationships with others can have a profound impact on our mental and emotional well-being, our motivation, and even our ability to reach our goals. In this chapter, we will explore why healthy relationships are so important and how to cultivate them in our lives.

Why Healthy Relationships Matter:

Humans are social creatures, and we thrive on connection with others. Healthy relationships provide us with a sense of belonging, support, and intimacy. They can help us feel understood, accepted, and loved. When we have healthy relationships, we are less likely to feel lonely or isolated, and we are better able to manage stress and other challenges.

In addition to their emotional benefits, healthy relationships can also contribute to our success in practical ways. They can provide us with networking opportunities, emotional support during difficult times, and valuable feedback on our ideas and projects. People with strong relationships tend to have better mental health, lower rates of chronic illness, and greater life satisfaction.

Building Healthy Relationships:

While healthy relationships may seem like they come naturally to some people, they are actually built through intentional effort and communication. Here are some tips for cultivating healthy relationships in your life:

- Be yourself: Authenticity is key to building healthy relationships. Be honest about your thoughts, feelings, and values, and allow others to do the same.
- Practice empathy: Try to understand others' perspectives and experiences, and respond with compassion and understanding.
- Communicate effectively: Healthy relationships rely on open, honest communication. Practice active listening, ask for clarification when needed, and express yourself clearly and respectfully.
- Set boundaries: Boundaries are important for maintaining healthy relationships. Be clear about your own boundaries and respect others' boundaries as well.
- Be reliable: Follow through on your commitments and be dependable. This helps build trust in your relationships.
- Express gratitude: Show appreciation for the people in your life and the things they do for you. This can help strengthen your connections and build positive feelings between you.

Nurturing Existing Relationships:

If you already have relationships in your life, it's important to nurture them to keep them healthy and strong. Here are some ways to do that:

- Stay in touch: Make an effort to stay connected with the people in your life, whether that's through regular check-ins, phone calls, or in-person visits.

- Show up: When the people in your life need support, be there for them. This can be as simple as listening to them when they need to vent or celebrating their successes with them.
- Practice forgiveness: No relationship is perfect, and conflicts and misunderstandings are bound to happen. Practice forgiveness and work through conflicts in a healthy way to maintain your connections.
- Keep it fresh: Even long-term relationships can benefit from novelty and spontaneity. Try new activities or hobbies together, or plan surprise outings or events to keep things interesting.

Cultivating New Relationships:

If you're looking to build new relationships in your life, there are many ways to do so. Here are some ideas:

- Join groups: Look for groups or organizations that align with your interests and values. This can be a great way to meet like-minded people and build connections.
- Volunteer: Volunteering is not only a great way to give back, but it can also help you meet new people and build relationships.
- Attend events: Attend events and activities in your community to meet new people and expand your social circle.
- Take classes: Whether it's a cooking class, a yoga class, or a language class, taking classes can help you meet new people who share your interests.

Communicating Effectively

Effective communication is a critical skill to master in order to achieve success in life. It can help you build strong relationships, foster understanding, and achieve your goals. In this chapter, we will explore the various aspects of effective communication and how you can improve your communication skills.

Listening is a key component of effective communication. When you listen actively, you show respect for the other person and demonstrate your interest in what they have to say. You can practice active listening by maintaining eye contact, nodding your head, and asking questions to clarify their message. Reflecting back on what the other person said and summarizing it in your own words can also help ensure that you understand their message.

Another important aspect of effective communication is being aware of your body language. Nonverbal cues such as facial expressions, posture, and tone of voice can convey a lot of information about how you are feeling and what you are thinking. To communicate effectively, try to maintain an open and relaxed posture, make eye contact, and use a calm and confident tone of voice.

When it comes to expressing your own thoughts and ideas, clarity is key. Be clear about your message and use simple language to convey your ideas. It can be helpful to organize your thoughts beforehand and have a clear idea of what you want to say.

In addition to clarity, it's also important to be aware of your audience. Consider who you are speaking to and adjust your message accordingly. For example, you may need to use different language or provide additional context when speaking to someone who is less familiar with the topic.

It's also important to be respectful and considerate when communicating with others. Avoid interrupting, speaking over others, or belittling their ideas. Instead, aim to find common ground and build a shared understanding.

Finally, it's important to be open to feedback and willing to learn from others. If you receive criticism or feedback, try to take it as an opportunity to grow and improve. Take the time to reflect on what was said, and consider how you can apply the feedback to improve your communication skills.

When I first started my job, I struggled with communicating effectively with my colleagues. I found it difficult to express my ideas clearly and was often misunderstood. However, after attending a communication workshop, I learned the importance of active listening, clarity, and respect. I started practicing these skills, and soon I noticed a significant improvement in my ability to communicate with others. I received positive feedback from my colleagues and felt more confident in expressing my ideas.

Resolving Conflict and Forgiveness

Resolving conflict and practicing forgiveness are crucial skills in maintaining healthy relationships. It's inevitable that we will encounter disagreements and misunderstandings with those around us, but knowing how to handle them can make all the difference in maintaining positive relationships.

First, it's important to acknowledge and express your own feelings about the situation, while also listening to the other person's perspective without judgment. Active listening involves paying attention to what the other person is saying and feeling, and responding with empathy and understanding.

Next, it's important to identify the source of the conflict and work together to find a resolution. This may involve compromise, finding a common ground, or simply agreeing to disagree. It's important to approach the situation with an open mind and a willingness to find a solution that works for everyone involved.

Forgiveness is also an important part of resolving conflict and maintaining healthy relationships. Holding onto anger and resentment can lead to further conflict and strain on relationships. Forgiveness involves letting go of the negative feelings associated with the situation and moving forward in a positive direction.

It's important to note that forgiveness does not necessarily mean forgetting the situation or condoning the other person's actions. It simply means acknowledging the situation and making a choice to let go of negative emotions and move forward in a positive direction.

Practicing forgiveness can be difficult, especially in situations where the other person may not have apologized or taken responsibility for their actions. However, forgiveness is ultimately a choice that we make for ourselves, in order to release ourselves from the burden of negative emotions and move forward in a positive direction.

In my own life, I have experienced the power of forgiveness in maintaining healthy relationships. There have been times when I have held onto anger and resentment towards someone, only to realize that it was ultimately hurting myself more than anyone else. By practicing forgiveness and letting go of those negative emotions, I was able to move forward in a positive direction and maintain a healthy relationship with the other person.

Overall, the ability to resolve conflict and practice forgiveness are important skills in maintaining healthy relationships. By approaching disagreements with empathy and understanding, identifying the source of conflict, and working together to find a resolution, we can maintain positive relationships and move forward in a positive direction.

Cultivating Emotional Intelligence

Understanding and Managing Emotions

Understanding and managing emotions is a crucial aspect of winning in life. Emotions can motivate us, but they can also hinder our progress if we don't know how to manage them. In this chapter, we will explore the importance of understanding and managing our emotions.

Emotions are a fundamental part of our human experience. We feel emotions every day, from happiness and joy to anger and sadness. However, not everyone is comfortable with their emotions or knows how to manage them effectively. Some people may even try to ignore or suppress their emotions, which can lead to negative consequences in their personal and professional lives.

The first step in understanding and managing emotions is to recognize and acknowledge them. This means identifying what we are feeling and why we are feeling it. For example, if we feel angry, we need to ask ourselves why we are feeling angry. Is it because of something someone said or did? Is it because we are frustrated with a situation? Understanding the root cause of our emotions can help us manage them more effectively.

Once we have identified our emotions, the next step is to manage them. This involves regulating our emotions so that we can respond appropriately to a given situation. For example, if we are feeling angry, we might take a few deep breaths or go for a walk to calm ourselves down before responding to the situation. We might also try to reframe the situation in a more positive light or practice empathy to understand the other person's perspective.

Managing emotions also involves developing emotional intelligence. This means being aware of our own emotions and the emotions of others, and being able to regulate our responses accordingly. Emotional intelligence can help us build better relationships, communicate more effectively, and make better decisions.

In my own life, I have found that understanding and managing my emotions has been a critical factor in my success. I used to struggle with anxiety and often felt overwhelmed by my emotions. However, through therapy and self-reflection, I learned how to identify and manage my emotions more effectively. This has allowed me to be more present in my relationships, communicate more effectively at work, and make better decisions in all areas of my life.

In conclusion, understanding and managing emotions is a crucial aspect of winning in life. By acknowledging and regulating our emotions, developing emotional intelligence, and practicing self-reflection, we can become more successful in all areas of our lives.

Empathy and Compassion

Empathy and compassion are essential traits that can greatly enhance our personal and professional relationships. When we understand and connect with the feelings and experiences of others, we can build deeper and more meaningful relationships, and even positively impact the world around us.

To start, empathy is the ability to understand and share the feelings of another person. Compassion is the feeling of concern for the suffering or misfortune of others, and the desire to help alleviate it.

Practicing empathy and compassion can have a profound impact on our personal and professional relationships. When we take the time to understand the perspectives and experiences of others, we can build deeper connections and trust, and foster more positive interactions.

To develop empathy and compassion, it's important to start by being present and attentive in our interactions with others. This means actively listening to what someone is saying, and trying to understand their perspective without judgment or assumptions. We can also practice putting ourselves in other people's shoes by imagining how we would feel in their situation.

Another important aspect of empathy and compassion is recognizing and validating the emotions of others. This means acknowledging and accepting their feelings, even if we don't necessarily agree with them or understand them completely. Validating someone's emotions can help them feel heard and understood, and can foster a deeper sense of connection and trust.

Compassion, on the other hand, involves taking action to help alleviate the suffering or misfortune of others. This can take many forms, from offering emotional support to actively helping someone in need. The key is to approach these situations with a genuine desire to help, and to do so in a way that respects the other person's autonomy and dignity.

Practicing empathy and compassion can be challenging at times, especially when we are dealing with difficult or emotionally charged situations. It's important to remember that these are skills that can be developed and improved over time with practice and intention.

In my own life, I have seen the power of empathy and compassion firsthand. By taking the time to understand and connect with the feelings and experiences of others, I have been able to build deeper and more meaningful relationships, both personally and professionally. And by approaching difficult situations with empathy and compassion, I have been able to find solutions and resolutions that respect the needs and feelings of everyone involved.

Overall, empathy and compassion are powerful tools that can help us navigate our relationships and interactions with others in a more positive and meaningful way. By practicing these traits regularly, we can foster deeper connections, build trust and respect, and make a positive impact on the world around us.

Developing Social Awareness

Developing social awareness is a crucial aspect of winning in life. It means being able to understand and connect with people from different backgrounds, cultures, and perspectives. Social awareness helps you build strong relationships and networks, which are important for success in both personal and professional life.

Here are some key points to keep in mind when developing social awareness:

1. Practice Active Listening: One of the most important skills for social awareness is active listening. This means giving your full attention to the person speaking, and taking the time to understand their perspective.
2. Empathy: Being able to put yourself in someone else's shoes is a powerful tool for social awareness. When you understand and empathize with someone's feelings and emotions, it helps build trust and rapport.
3. Respect Diversity: Everyone is unique, and it's important to respect and celebrate those differences. By doing so, you can learn from different perspectives and gain a deeper understanding of the world around you.
4. Build Relationships: Social awareness is about building strong relationships with others. Take the time to connect with people on a personal level, and invest in those relationships over time.
5. Cultural Competence: It's important to have a basic understanding of different cultures and customs. This helps you avoid misunderstandings and build stronger relationships with people from diverse backgrounds.
6. Self-Awareness: Finally, self-awareness is an important component of social awareness. Knowing your own strengths and weaknesses, biases, and preferences can help you connect with others in a more authentic way.

Growing up, I was always interested in learning about different cultures and meeting new people. When I went to college, I joined a multicultural club and was able to connect with students from all over the world. Through this experience, I learned about different customs, beliefs, and perspectives, which helped me develop my social awareness. I also realized the importance of active listening and building strong relationships, both of which have been instrumental in my personal and professional life.

Investing in Yourself

Continual Learning and Personal Growth

Continual learning and personal growth are essential for long-term success and fulfillment in life. The world is constantly changing, and we need to adapt and grow with it. We need to continually learn and develop new skills and knowledge to remain relevant and competitive in our chosen fields. Additionally, personal growth involves developing our character, values, and attitudes to become the best version of ourselves. In this chapter, we will explore the importance of continual learning and personal growth and how to achieve it.

The Importance of Continual Learning: Learning is not something that ends when you graduate from school or university. In fact, it is just the beginning. Continual learning is crucial for personal and professional growth. Here are some reasons why:

1. Stay Relevant: The world is changing at an ever-increasing pace, and what is relevant today may not be relevant tomorrow. Continual learning allows you to stay up-to-date with the latest trends, developments, and technologies in your field.
2. Build Confidence: Learning new skills and knowledge gives you a sense of accomplishment and builds confidence. As you develop new skills, you become more competent, which enhances your self-esteem.
3. Enhance Creativity: Learning new things can inspire creativity and innovation. Exposure to new ideas, perspectives, and experiences can spark your imagination and help you think outside the box.

4. Keep Your Brain Active: Learning is good for your brain health. It helps to keep your brain active and engaged, which can prevent cognitive decline as you age.

The Importance of Personal Growth: Personal growth is about developing yourself as a person, beyond your skills and knowledge. It involves enhancing your character, values, and attitudes to become the best version of yourself. Here are some reasons why personal growth is important:

1. Increase Self-awareness: Personal growth helps you to develop self-awareness, which is the foundation for personal and professional success. When you are aware of your strengths, weaknesses, and values, you can make better decisions and be more effective in your personal and professional life.
2. Improve Relationships: Personal growth can help you to build better relationships with others. When you have a greater understanding of yourself, you are better able to empathize with others and communicate effectively with them.
3. Enhance Resilience: Personal growth can help you to develop resilience, which is the ability to bounce back from setbacks and challenges. When you have a growth mindset, you view challenges as opportunities for learning and growth.
4. Increase Fulfillment: Personal growth can lead to greater fulfillment and satisfaction in life. When you are living in alignment with your values and purpose, you feel more fulfilled and happy.

Strategies for Continual Learning and Personal Growth:

1. Read: Reading is a great way to learn new things and expand your knowledge. Make a habit of reading books, articles, and blogs related to your interests and professional development.
2. Attend Workshops and Seminars: Workshops and seminars are a great way to learn new skills and connect with others in your field. Look for workshops and seminars that are relevant to your interests and attend them regularly.
3. Take Online Courses: There are many online courses available that can help you to develop new skills and knowledge. Look for courses that are relevant to your interests and professional development.
4. Seek Feedback: Ask for feedback from colleagues, mentors, and friends to help you identify areas for improvement and opportunities for growth.
5. Reflect: Take time to reflect on your experiences and what you have learned from them. This can help you to identify areas for improvement and to develop a growth mindset.
6. Step Outside Your Comfort Zone: To grow, you need to step outside your comfort zone and take on new challenges. Look for opportunities to stretch yourself and take risks.

Self-Care and Well-Being

Self-care and well-being are crucial aspects of leading a successful and fulfilling life. Often, we get so busy with our work and responsibilities that we forget to take care of ourselves. However, neglecting our physical, emotional, and mental health can have long-term consequences that can hinder our personal and professional growth. In this chapter, we'll explore the importance of self-care and well-being and some strategies to incorporate them into your daily life.

Taking care of your physical health is the foundation of self-care. It includes getting enough sleep, eating healthy foods, exercising regularly, and avoiding unhealthy habits such as smoking or excessive drinking. When we neglect our physical health, it can lead to a host of issues such as chronic illnesses, fatigue, and mental health problems such as anxiety and depression. Making small changes in your daily routine such as taking a walk after dinner, incorporating fruits and vegetables into your meals, or prioritizing a good night's sleep can make a significant difference in how you feel both physically and mentally.

Emotional well-being is equally important. We all experience ups and downs in life, but it's important to be able to manage our emotions in a healthy way. Practicing mindfulness and meditation can help you stay centered and calm in the face of adversity. Building a support network of friends and family can provide a source of emotional support during difficult times. If you find that your emotions are interfering with your daily life, seeking the help of a mental health professional can be beneficial.

Personal growth also involves taking time for hobbies, interests, and relaxation. Engaging in activities that bring you joy can help reduce stress and improve overall well-being. Whether it's reading a book, playing a musical instrument, or practicing a sport, carving out time for things that make you happy is crucial for self-care.

Finally, self-care also means knowing when to take a break and step back from work and responsibilities. It's easy to fall into the trap of feeling like we always have to be productive, but taking breaks and allowing ourselves to rest is just as important. Whether it's taking a day off from work, going on a vacation, or simply spending an evening relaxing at home, it's essential to prioritize rest and relaxation.

In my own life, I've learned the hard way that neglecting self-care can have serious consequences. There have been times when I've pushed myself too hard and neglected my physical and emotional health, leading to burnout and mental health issues. Through trial and error, I've learned that taking care of myself isn't selfish, but rather, it's necessary for me to be able to show up as my best self in all areas of my life.

In conclusion, self-care and well-being are crucial aspects of personal growth and success. Prioritizing your physical, emotional, and mental health, taking time for hobbies and relaxation, and knowing when to take a break are all strategies that can help you lead a more fulfilling and satisfying life. Remember, taking care of yourself isn't selfish, it's essential for your personal and professional growth.

Finding Balance and Managing Stress

In today's fast-paced and constantly changing world, finding balance and managing stress can be a challenge. It's essential to take care of yourself, both mentally and physically, to avoid burnout and to live a fulfilling life. In this chapter, we'll explore some strategies for finding balance and managing stress.

Managing Stress:

Stress is a part of life, and it can come from many sources, including work, relationships, finances, health problems, and more. While it's impossible to eliminate stress completely, there are ways to manage it effectively.

One effective way to manage stress is to identify the source of the stress and find ways to minimize it. For example, if your job is causing you a lot of stress, consider talking to your boss about ways to reduce your workload or to find more support. If you're feeling stressed because of financial issues, consider making a budget or talking to a financial advisor. In some cases, it may be necessary to make bigger changes, such as switching jobs or moving to a new city.

Another way to manage stress is through physical activity. Exercise has been shown to be an effective way to reduce stress levels and improve overall health. You don't have to become a marathon runner to benefit from exercise; even a short walk or gentle yoga session can help to reduce stress.

Meditation and mindfulness practices can also be helpful in managing stress. These practices involve focusing on the present moment and letting go of worries about the past or future. They can help to reduce stress and improve overall well-being.

Finding Balance:

Finding balance is about taking care of yourself and ensuring that you're devoting enough time and energy to all aspects of your life. This includes your work, relationships, hobbies, and self-care.

One way to find balance is to prioritize your time. Make a list of your top priorities and ensure that you're devoting enough time and energy to each one. For example, if spending time with your family is a top priority, ensure that you're scheduling regular family time and saying no to other commitments that conflict with this time.

Another way to find balance is to practice self-care. Self-care involves taking care of yourself mentally and physically. This can include getting enough sleep, eating a healthy diet, engaging in physical activity, and taking time for yourself to relax and recharge.

It's also important to set boundaries and say no when necessary. Saying yes to everything can lead to burnout and overwhelm. Setting boundaries and saying no can help you to prioritize your time and energy and ensure that you're not taking on too much.

I used to struggle with finding balance and managing stress. I would often take on too much at work and neglect my relationships and hobbies. As a result, I would feel overwhelmed and burnt out. I decided to make some changes in my life to prioritize my well-being.

I started by setting boundaries at work and saying no to projects that would require me to work long hours or to take on too much responsibility. I also started prioritizing my relationships and hobbies by scheduling regular time for these activities. I found that taking time for myself and engaging in activities that I enjoyed helped to reduce my stress levels and improve my overall well-being.

Overall, finding balance and managing stress requires ongoing effort and a commitment to self-care. By identifying sources of stress, practicing stress-management techniques, prioritizing your time, and engaging in self-care, you can find balance and live a fulfilling life.

Taking Risks

Overcoming Fear and Doubt

Fear and doubt are common emotions that can hold us back from achieving our goals and living the life we want. Whether it's a fear of failure, rejection, or the unknown, these feelings can paralyze us and prevent us from taking action. However, it's important to recognize that fear and doubt are normal and that everyone experiences them at some point in their lives.

One of the first steps in overcoming fear and doubt is to acknowledge them. It's important to understand that these emotions are not necessarily based on reality, but rather our perception of reality. For example, the fear of public speaking is a common fear, but it's not necessarily based on any real danger. By acknowledging our fears and doubts, we can start to examine them more objectively and challenge them.

Another important step in overcoming fear and doubt is to take action. Often, we may feel stuck because we don't know what to do or where to start. However, taking even small steps towards our goals can help us build confidence and overcome our fears. For example, if you have a fear of public speaking, you could start by practicing your presentation in front of a small group of friends or family members.

It's also important to surround ourselves with positive and supportive people. Having a support system can help us build confidence and overcome our fears. Seek out friends, family members, or colleagues who believe in you and encourage you to pursue your goals. These people can help you stay motivated and remind you of your strengths and abilities when you're feeling doubt.

In addition, it's important to practice self-compassion. We are often our own harshest critics, and it's easy to fall into a cycle of negative self-talk when we're feeling fearful or doubtful. However, treating ourselves with kindness and understanding can help us build resilience and overcome our fears. When we make mistakes or face setbacks, it's important to remind ourselves that it's okay to be imperfect and that we can learn and grow from our experiences.

Finally, it's important to recognize that overcoming fear and doubt is a process, and it's okay to take things one step at a time. We may not conquer our fears overnight, but with patience, persistence, and self-compassion, we can build the resilience we need to face them head-on.

Personally, I have struggled with fear and doubt at various points in my life. One example was when I decided to pursue a career change and return to school for a graduate degree. I was filled with doubt about whether I could handle the academic workload, whether I was making the right decision, and whether I would be able to find a job in my new field. However, I acknowledged my fears and doubts and sought support from family and friends. I also took small steps, such as attending information sessions and reaching out to alumni in my new field, which helped me build confidence and overcome my fears. Eventually, I was able to graduate with honors and find a job in my new field that I love.

Calculated Risk-Taking

Calculated risk-taking is an essential element of success, but it can also be scary and daunting. The idea of taking a chance on something with no guaranteed outcome can be terrifying, especially when failure is a possible result. However, if you want to achieve your goals and reach your full potential, taking calculated risks is a must.

Calculated risk-taking is all about weighing the potential risks and rewards of a particular decision and making a conscious and informed choice to move forward based on that analysis. It's not about being reckless or impulsive, but rather about being strategic and thoughtful in your decision-making.

One of the biggest benefits of calculated risk-taking is that it allows you to expand your comfort zone and push beyond your limits. When you take calculated risks, you're stretching yourself and challenging yourself to grow and learn in new ways. This can be incredibly empowering and can lead to increased confidence and self-esteem.

Of course, there's always the possibility of failure when taking a calculated risk. But even in the event of failure, there are lessons to be learned and opportunities for growth. In fact, some of the greatest successes in history have come as a result of failures or setbacks along the way.

To take calculated risks effectively, you need to have a clear understanding of your goals and values. You should also be well-informed about the risks involved and have a solid plan in place for how you'll mitigate those risks and move forward if things don't go as planned.

It's also important to trust yourself and your instincts when it comes to taking calculated risks. Don't be afraid to listen to your gut, even if it goes against conventional wisdom or the opinions of others.

In my own life, I've had to take several calculated risks to get to where I am today. One of the biggest risks I took was leaving a stable job to start my own business. I knew the risks involved, but I also knew that I had a solid plan and was passionate about what I was doing. Though there were certainly challenges and setbacks along the way, that decision ultimately led to great success and personal fulfillment.

In conclusion, calculated risk-taking is an important element of success and personal growth. While it can be scary, the potential rewards make it well worth the effort. By weighing the risks and rewards, having a clear plan, and trusting yourself, you can take calculated risks that propel you toward your goals and help you reach your full potential.

Embracing Failure and Learning from Mistakes

Failure is an inevitable part of life. No matter how hard we try, sometimes things just don't work out the way we want them to. But instead of letting failure bring us down, we can use it as an opportunity for growth and learning. In fact, many successful people credit their failures as a key factor in their eventual success.

One of the most important things we can do when faced with failure is to embrace it. It's natural to want to avoid failure, but by doing so, we may miss out on valuable lessons and experiences. Instead, we can choose to see failure as a teacher, helping us learn what doesn't work so we can make adjustments and try again.

It's also important to learn from our mistakes. After experiencing failure, it's easy to fall into a cycle of self-blame and negative self-talk. But by reframing our thinking and approaching failure with a growth mindset, we can use our mistakes as opportunities to learn and improve.

For example, when I first started my own business, I made a lot of mistakes. I lost money on investments, made poor decisions about hiring and management, and struggled to gain traction in a competitive market. At the time, these failures felt devastating. But as I reflected on my experiences and sought out advice from others, I realized that each mistake was a valuable lesson. I learned about the importance of market research, the need for effective communication with employees, and the value of persistence and perseverance.

Another key factor in overcoming failure is to avoid being overly hard on ourselves. It's important to recognize that failure is a natural part of growth and development, and that we all make mistakes. By practicing self-compassion and focusing on what we can learn from our failures, we can move forward with greater resilience and confidence.

Ultimately, the key to embracing failure is to approach it with a growth mindset. Instead of seeing failures as evidence of our limitations, we can view them as opportunities for growth and learning. By staying curious, open-minded, and willing to take risks, we can turn our failures into stepping stones on the path to success.

Seeking and Accepting Help

The Power of Asking for Help

Asking for help can be a difficult thing to do, but it is an incredibly powerful tool in achieving success. It takes a certain amount of vulnerability to admit that you don't have all the answers or that you need assistance, but once you do, you open yourself up to a wealth of resources and knowledge.

Personally, I used to struggle with asking for help. I believed that asking for help meant that I was weak or that I wasn't capable of handling things on my own. But as I began to face more complex challenges in my life, I realized that there was only so much I could do alone. I started to see that asking for help wasn't a sign of weakness, but a sign of strength and wisdom.

One of the most powerful benefits of asking for help is that it expands your knowledge and resources. There are countless people in the world who have more experience or knowledge in a particular area than we do. By seeking out their help, we can learn from their expertise and gain a deeper understanding of the subject matter. For example, if you're trying to learn a new skill or subject, seeking out a mentor or teacher can be an incredibly valuable resource.

Asking for help also helps us to avoid making unnecessary mistakes. When we try to tackle everything on our own, we're bound to make errors or overlook important details. But by asking for help, we can catch those mistakes before they become larger problems. This can save us time, money, and stress in the long run.

It's important to note that asking for help isn't a one-way street. When we ask for help, we also have the opportunity to give back to those who have helped us. This creates a sense of community and connection, which is essential to our personal growth and success.

Of course, asking for help can still be intimidating, especially if you're afraid of being rejected or judged. But it's important to remember that most people are more than happy to help when they can. If someone can't help you, it's not a reflection of your worth or ability. It simply means that they may not have the knowledge or resources to assist you at that moment.

In conclusion, asking for help is an essential tool for personal and professional growth. It allows us to expand our knowledge and resources, avoid unnecessary mistakes, and build valuable connections. Don't be afraid to ask for help when you need it. Remember, it's a sign of strength and wisdom, not weakness.

Building a Support System

Building a support system is a crucial aspect of personal growth and success. No one can achieve their goals alone, and having a strong support system can make all the difference. A support system can provide encouragement, guidance, and emotional support when needed.

When building a support system, it is essential to identify the people who will provide the necessary support. These people can be family members, friends, mentors, or coaches. It is important to choose people who are trustworthy, supportive, and will hold you accountable.

One of the most important elements of a support system is having people who will believe in you, even when you don't believe in yourself. These people will help you see your strengths and abilities, and will encourage you to keep going even when you face setbacks.

Another crucial aspect of building a support system is being willing to ask for help. Many people struggle with asking for help, either because they don't want to burden others or because they feel embarrassed or ashamed. However, asking for help is a sign of strength, not weakness. It takes courage to admit that you need assistance, and it shows that you are willing to take action to achieve your goals.

It is also important to be willing to offer support to others in your support system. Supporting others can help strengthen your relationships and build a sense of community. When you provide support to others, you are showing that you value their goals and are willing to help them achieve them.

When building a support system, it is important to be intentional and proactive. You can start by identifying the people in your life who are supportive and encouraging. You can also seek out mentors, coaches, or support groups that align with your values and goals.

In my own experience, building a support system has been essential for my personal and professional growth. I have found that having people in my life who believe in me and encourage me to pursue my goals has been instrumental in helping me achieve success. I have also learned that being willing to ask for help when I need it is a sign of strength, and that providing support to others is just as important as receiving it. By building a strong support system, you can create a network of people who will help you achieve your goals and be there for you during both the successes and the setbacks.

Being Grateful and Giving Back

Being grateful and giving back to others are essential components of a fulfilling life. When we express gratitude and give back to others, we cultivate a sense of purpose and happiness that cannot be found through personal achievement alone.

Expressing gratitude is one of the most powerful things we can do for ourselves and for others. When we take the time to acknowledge and appreciate the people and things in our lives, we begin to see the world through a lens of abundance rather than scarcity. Gratitude helps us to focus on what we have rather than what we lack, and it allows us to build stronger relationships with the people in our lives.

One way to cultivate gratitude is to start a daily gratitude practice. This can be as simple as taking a few minutes each day to write down three things that you are grateful for. These things can be big or small, but they should be specific. For example, instead of writing "I'm grateful for my family," you might write, "I'm grateful for my sister's sense of humor that always makes me laugh."

Giving back to others is another way to cultivate a sense of purpose and happiness. When we give back, we not only help those in need, but we also benefit ourselves. Helping others can boost our self-esteem, increase our sense of connection to others, and give us a sense of purpose.

There are countless ways to give back to others, both in our local communities and on a larger scale. We might volunteer at a local food bank or animal shelter, make a donation to a charity that we believe in, or simply take the time to listen to a friend in need.

Personally, I have found that volunteering at my local homeless shelter has been an incredibly rewarding experience. I've had the opportunity to meet people from all walks of life and hear their stories. By simply listening and showing compassion, I've been able to make a small but meaningful difference in their lives.

In conclusion, expressing gratitude and giving back to others are essential components of a fulfilling life. By cultivating these practices, we can find greater purpose and happiness in our daily lives and make a positive impact on the world around us.

Persevering Through Challenges

The Power of Persistence

Persistence is the key to achieving anything worthwhile in life. It's the ability to keep going despite setbacks, obstacles, and challenges. When we face difficulties, it can be easy to give up and walk away, but it's important to remember that success often comes to those who are willing to persevere.

Personally, I've experienced the power of persistence in my own life. When I was in college, I had a dream of studying abroad in Spain, but I faced numerous obstacles along the way. I had to work multiple jobs to save up enough money to pay for the trip, and I struggled to find the right program and get accepted.

However, I refused to give up on my dream. I kept working hard, researching programs, and applying until I finally found a program that was a good fit. I was accepted and ended up spending an incredible semester studying abroad in Spain.

This experience taught me the importance of persistence in achieving our goals. Without the willingness to keep going despite setbacks and obstacles, I would never have achieved my dream of studying abroad.

When it comes to achieving our goals, it's important to remember that setbacks and failures are part of the journey. It's how we respond to those setbacks that matters. Instead of giving up, we must use them as learning opportunities and keep pushing forward.

Another personal example of persistence in my life is in my career. When I first started out, I faced numerous rejections and setbacks in my job search. It was tempting to give up and settle for a job that wasn't fulfilling, but I knew that wasn't what I wanted for myself.

So, I kept applying, networking, and developing my skills until I finally landed a job that was a perfect fit for me. Without the willingness to persist, I would never have achieved my goals in my career.

In order to cultivate persistence, it's important to have a strong sense of purpose and motivation. When we have a clear goal in mind, we are more likely to keep going despite setbacks. It's also helpful to break our goals down into smaller, manageable steps, so that we can feel a sense of progress along the way.

It's important to remember that persistence is not the same as stubbornness. While it's important to stay committed to our goals, we must also be willing to adapt and make changes when necessary. Sometimes, the best way to achieve our goals is to take a different approach.

In conclusion, persistence is a vital trait for achieving our goals and fulfilling our dreams. With a strong sense of purpose and motivation, and a willingness to adapt and learn from setbacks, we can cultivate the power of persistence in our own lives.

Dealing with Setbacks and Failure

Setbacks and failure are inevitable in life, especially when we are trying to achieve our goals and pursue our dreams. While it can be disheartening to experience failure, it is important to remember that it is a natural part of the learning process and an opportunity for growth and development.

Dealing with setbacks and failure can be challenging, but there are strategies that can help us overcome these obstacles and keep moving forward.

First, it is important to take time to process our emotions and reactions to failure. It is natural to feel disappointed, frustrated, or even angry when things do not go as planned. Acknowledging these emotions and allowing ourselves to feel them can be an important step in moving forward.

Next, it is important to reflect on the situation and try to identify what went wrong and why. This can help us learn from the experience and make changes to our approach in the future. It is important to be honest with ourselves and take responsibility for our role in the failure, while also recognizing external factors that may have contributed to the outcome.

It can also be helpful to seek feedback from others who were involved in the situation or who may have expertise in the area. This feedback can provide valuable insights and perspectives that we may not have considered on our own.

Once we have processed our emotions and reflected on the situation, it is important to take action and make a plan for moving forward. This may involve adjusting our goals, reevaluating our strategies, or seeking additional support or resources.

It is also important to maintain a positive mindset and focus on the lessons learned and opportunities for growth that come from failure. It can be easy to become discouraged and give up on our goals after experiencing failure, but persistence and a growth mindset can help us continue to move forward despite setbacks.

Personally, I have experienced setbacks and failure in various areas of my life, including academics, relationships, and career. While these experiences were challenging at the time, they have ultimately taught me valuable lessons and helped me grow as a person. For example, when I failed an important exam in college, I was devastated and felt like a failure. However, I took time to reflect on what went wrong and adjusted my study habits for future exams. Ultimately, I was able to improve my grades and achieve my academic goals.

In conclusion, setbacks and failure are a natural part of life, but with the right mindset and strategies, we can overcome these obstacles and continue to work towards our goals. By taking time to process our emotions, reflect on the situation, seek feedback, and take action, we can turn failure into an opportunity for growth and development.

Finding Hope and Strength in Difficult Times

Life can be unpredictable and challenging, and at times it may seem like we're facing insurmountable obstacles. Whether it's the loss of a loved one, a health issue, or a personal setback, difficult times can test our strength and resilience. But even in the darkest moments, there is always hope and strength to be found. In this chapter, we'll explore ways to find hope and strength when facing adversity.

First and foremost, it's important to acknowledge and accept the situation you're in. It's normal to feel overwhelmed, scared, or even hopeless in difficult times. Instead of denying or ignoring your feelings, try to sit with them and process them. This may involve talking to a trusted friend or family member, seeking professional help, or engaging in self-care activities like meditation, exercise, or journaling.

In difficult times, it's also important to focus on the present moment and take things one step at a time. It's easy to get caught up in worrying about the future or dwelling on the past, but this can make things feel even more overwhelming. Instead, try to stay present and focus on what you can do right now to move forward.

Another helpful strategy is to find sources of hope and inspiration. This could be a quote that resonates with you, a person who inspires you, or a story of someone who overcame a similar challenge. Surrounding yourself with positive influences can help you stay motivated and remind you that you're not alone.

In addition to finding hope, it's important to tap into your inner strength. Even if you don't feel strong right now, remember that you've overcome challenges before and you can do it again. Try to identify your personal strengths and values, and draw on these to help you navigate difficult times.

It's also important to recognize that asking for help is a sign of strength, not weakness. Whether it's seeking professional help, reaching out to friends and family, or joining a support group, connecting with others can provide a valuable source of comfort and encouragement.

Finally, it's important to remember that difficult times can also provide opportunities for growth and self-discovery. While it may not feel like it in the moment, going through challenges can help you develop resilience, empathy, and a deeper understanding of yourself and others. By embracing the journey and staying hopeful, you can emerge from difficult times stronger and more resilient than ever before.

Personally, I have faced my share of difficult times, including the loss of a loved one and personal setbacks. During these times, I found it helpful to lean on my support system and engage in self-care activities like meditation and exercise. I also found inspiration in stories of people who overcame adversity and reminded myself of my own strengths and values. While it wasn't easy, these strategies helped me find hope and strength during challenging times.

Maintaining Integrity and Values

Ethics and Integrity in Success

Ethics and integrity are vital components of success. Success, when achieved with integrity, gives one the satisfaction and fulfillment that cannot be found in shortcuts or dishonesty. Acting with integrity means adhering to a set of moral principles, such as honesty, fairness, and responsibility, while ethics is the study of how people should behave in a moral sense.

At times, individuals can be tempted to bend or even break ethical principles to get ahead or achieve success. However, this can lead to a short-lived success that is often overshadowed by the consequences of unethical behavior. Ethical lapses can damage relationships, destroy trust, and even result in legal and financial consequences. The consequences of unethical actions may not always be immediate, but they will eventually catch up.

Having a strong moral compass and following ethical guidelines is not only the right thing to do but also pays off in the long run. When people act with integrity, they earn respect, trust, and a positive reputation. Ethical behavior also promotes a healthy work culture, where everyone feels valued and respected.

I recall a time when I was working in a retail store during college, and I witnessed an act of dishonesty by one of my coworkers. They had pocketed money from a customer's purchase and thought they had gotten away with it. However, they were eventually caught, and their actions not only resulted in their termination but also damaged the store's reputation. The store lost business, and many customers no longer trusted the employees.

On the other hand, I have also witnessed individuals who have achieved great success while acting with integrity. They made sure to follow ethical guidelines in their business practices, treated their employees fairly, and made sure to give back to their community. These individuals have built strong reputations, earned the respect of others, and continue to experience sustained success.

In conclusion, ethics and integrity are crucial components of success that should never be compromised. Success achieved through unethical means is often short-lived and can lead to serious consequences. On the other hand, success achieved with integrity brings satisfaction, fulfillment, and a positive reputation. By acting with integrity and adhering to ethical principles, individuals can build a strong foundation for success that will last.

Staying True to Your Values

Staying true to your values is essential to living a fulfilling and meaningful life. Our values shape who we are, our priorities, and the way we interact with the world around us. They guide our decisions and actions, and they reflect what we stand for. When we are true to our values, we feel a sense of purpose and integrity, which is essential for our well-being.

Identifying our values is the first step to staying true to them. Our values can be shaped by our upbringing, our culture, our personal experiences, and our beliefs. Some of the most common values include honesty, respect, compassion, loyalty, justice, and excellence. However, everyone's values are unique, and it's important to identify what matters most to us personally.

Staying true to our values can be challenging, especially in situations where we feel pressured to compromise them. For example, we might be tempted to cheat or lie to get ahead in our careers, or we might be asked to do something that goes against our moral principles. In such situations, it's important to take a step back and reflect on our values. We can ask ourselves, "Is this consistent with who I am and what I stand for?" If the answer is no, then we need to find the courage to say no and stay true to ourselves.

Staying true to our values also requires us to be mindful of our actions and their impact on others. It's easy to get caught up in our own needs and desires, but we must remember that our actions can have a ripple effect on the people around us. For example, if we value honesty, we need to be honest not only with ourselves but also with others. We need to be aware of the impact of our words and actions on those around us.

Staying true to our values is not always easy, but it's essential for living a fulfilling and meaningful life. When we are true to ourselves and our values, we feel a sense of purpose and fulfillment that cannot be found elsewhere. We become better versions of ourselves, and we inspire others to do the same.

Personally, staying true to my values has been a journey of self-discovery and growth. When I was younger, I struggled with the pressure to conform to the expectations of others, even if it meant compromising my own values.

However, over time, I realized that being true to myself was more important than pleasing others. I learned to identify my values, stand up for what I believed in, and surround myself with people who shared my values. As a result, I have been able to live a more authentic and fulfilling life, and I hope to continue doing so in the years to come.

Building Trust and Reputation

Building trust and reputation is crucial for achieving long-term success in both personal and professional spheres. Trust and reputation are two of the most valuable assets that an individual or organization can possess. They take years to build but can be lost in a moment.

Trust is the foundation of all successful relationships, whether it is with family, friends, colleagues, or clients. When people trust you, they are more likely to work with you, share their ideas, and rely on you. On the other hand, a lack of trust can hinder progress and create barriers to communication.

Reputation, on the other hand, is the reflection of how people perceive you or your brand. It is a combination of your actions, behaviors, and the image you project to the world. A positive reputation can open doors, while a negative one can limit opportunities and harm relationships.

To build trust and reputation, it is essential to remain consistent in your actions and behaviors. Be honest, transparent, and reliable in your dealings with others. Keep your promises, follow through on commitments, and take responsibility for your mistakes. This will not only help build trust but also foster respect and admiration.

Maintaining a positive reputation requires being mindful of your actions both in public and in private. Your reputation can be impacted by your social media presence, the way you communicate, and the way you handle conflicts. It is essential to be aware of how you come across to others and be intentional about shaping your image.

One way to build trust and reputation is to prioritize open communication. This includes being receptive to feedback and actively seeking out ways to improve. Embrace transparency and be open about your intentions, goals, and motivations. This helps build credibility and strengthens relationships.

Another important aspect of building trust and reputation is demonstrating competence and expertise in your field. Be knowledgeable, stay up-to-date with the latest trends and developments, and continually seek opportunities to improve your skills and knowledge.

In summary, building trust and reputation takes time and effort, but it is worth it. It requires consistency in actions and behaviors, maintaining a positive image, open communication, and demonstrating expertise in your field. By doing so, you can build a strong foundation for success and long-lasting relationships.

Leaving a Legacy

Finding Meaning and Purpose in Life

Finding meaning and purpose in life is a universal human desire. We all want to feel that our lives have meaning and that we are contributing to something greater than ourselves. However, the path to finding meaning and purpose can be different for each person. In this subchapter, we will explore some of the ways you can find meaning and purpose in your life.

First, it is important to understand that meaning and purpose are not things that can be obtained like a material possession. Instead, they are a process of discovery and creation. It is up to each individual to find what resonates with them and what gives them a sense of purpose.

One way to begin this process is by exploring your passions and interests. What are the things that make you feel alive and energized? What activities do you lose track of time while doing? These are often indications of what you are most passionate about. By focusing on your passions and interests, you may find that you naturally gravitate towards activities that give you a sense of purpose.

Another way to find meaning and purpose is through service to others. Helping others can be deeply fulfilling and can give you a sense of connection and purpose. This can include volunteering in your community, helping a friend in need, or simply showing kindness to those around you. By focusing on the needs of others, you may find that you gain a deeper understanding of yourself and your own values.

In addition, it is important to reflect on your values and what you stand for. What are the things that you are most passionate about and believe in? This could include issues related to social justice, the environment, or education. By aligning your actions with your values, you can find a greater sense of purpose and meaning in your life.

It is also important to keep in mind that finding meaning and purpose is an ongoing process. It is not something that can be achieved overnight, but rather a journey of self-discovery and growth. As you go through different experiences and stages of life, your sense of purpose may shift and evolve. It is important to remain open to new experiences and to continue to explore your passions and interests.

Finally, finding meaning and purpose in life can also come from connecting with something greater than yourself. This can include spirituality, religion, or a sense of connection to the natural world. By connecting with something beyond yourself, you may find that you gain a greater sense of perspective and purpose.

In conclusion, finding meaning and purpose in life is a deeply personal journey. It requires self-reflection, exploration, and an openness to new experiences. By focusing on your passions, serving others, aligning your actions with your values, remaining open to new experiences, and connecting with something greater than yourself, you can find a sense of meaning and purpose that is uniquely your own.

Making a Positive Impact on the World

Making a positive impact on the world is a deeply personal and meaningful goal for many individuals. It's a noble aspiration that is rooted in the desire to contribute to something greater than oneself, and to leave the world a better place than how we found it.

When we think of making a positive impact on the world, it's natural to think of grandiose gestures such as solving world hunger or eradicating disease. However, making a positive impact can also be achieved through small actions that ripple outwards and create positive change in our immediate surroundings.

One of the most effective ways to make a positive impact on the world is to start with our own community. Volunteering for local organizations, donating to charities, and supporting small businesses are just a few examples of how we can help those around us. By taking these actions, we not only help others but also create a sense of unity and solidarity in our communities.

Another way to make a positive impact is to become an advocate for causes that we are passionate about. This can involve anything from raising awareness about environmental issues to promoting mental health awareness. Through advocacy, we can encourage others to join us in our efforts and create a larger movement for change.

Finally, it's important to remember that making a positive impact doesn't have to be limited to our personal lives. It's also possible to make a difference through our careers and professional pursuits. By using our skills and expertise to create products or services that benefit others, we can make a meaningful impact on a larger scale.

Ultimately, making a positive impact on the world is about finding ways to use our unique talents and resources to make a difference in the lives of others. It requires a willingness to take action, a commitment to our values, and a belief that even the smallest acts of kindness and compassion can create a better world for all.

Creating a Lasting Legacy

Creating a lasting legacy is something that many of us aspire to do. We want to make a positive impact on the world and leave behind something that will be remembered long after we're gone. While it can be easy to focus on short-term goals and immediate gratification, building a legacy requires a long-term perspective and a willingness to work hard and make sacrifices.

One of the first steps in creating a lasting legacy is to identify what you want to be remembered for. This can be a difficult task, as it requires you to think deeply about your values and the impact you want to have on the world. Some people may want to leave behind a physical monument or a piece of art, while others may want to be remembered for their philanthropy or social impact. Whatever it is that you want to be remembered for, it should be something that inspires you and motivates you to work towards it every day.

To build a lasting legacy, it's important to take action towards your goals every day. This means setting long-term goals, breaking them down into smaller steps, and consistently working towards them. It also means being willing to make sacrifices and stay focused on your goals, even when it's difficult or uncomfortable. For example, if you want to be remembered for your philanthropy, you may need to prioritize giving over personal luxuries or entertainment.

It's also important to recognize that building a lasting legacy is not a solo endeavor. It requires the support and collaboration of others, whether that's through building a team, partnering with like-minded individuals, or seeking out mentorship and guidance from those who have come before you. This means building strong relationships, treating others with respect and kindness, and being open to feedback and collaboration.

Creating a lasting legacy also requires a commitment to continual learning and growth. The world is constantly changing, and in order to stay relevant and effective, you must be willing to adapt and evolve with it. This means being open to new ideas and perspectives, seeking out opportunities for learning and development, and continually challenging yourself to improve.

Ultimately, creating a lasting legacy is about making a positive impact on the world and leaving behind something that will inspire and uplift others for generations to come. It's not an easy task, but with dedication, hard work, and a willingness to collaborate and learn, it's something that anyone can achieve.

Personally, I am inspired by the legacies of individuals like Mahatma Gandhi, Martin Luther King Jr., and Mother Teresa. These individuals dedicated their lives to fighting for justice and equality, and their legacies continue to inspire and motivate people around the world today. While I may not be able to achieve the same level of impact as these individuals, their stories remind me that creating a lasting legacy is possible, and that by working towards our goals with determination and compassion, we can make a difference in the world.

Conclusion

As we come to the end of this journey together, it is clear that success is not simply a matter of luck or talent, but a result of intentional actions and habits that we cultivate over time. We have explored a wide range of topics, from mindset and goal setting to interpersonal skills and ethical conduct. Each of these areas is crucial in its own right, and together they form a comprehensive framework for achieving success in all areas of life.

At the heart of this framework is the idea that success is not just about achieving our own personal goals, but about making a positive impact on the world around us. Whether it is through our work, our relationships, or our community involvement, we have the power to leave a lasting legacy that goes far beyond our own lifetime.

But achieving this kind of success is not easy. It requires a deep commitment to personal growth and development, a willingness to take risks and embrace failure, and a strong sense of purpose and meaning in life. It also requires us to be kind, compassionate, and empathetic towards ourselves and others, as we navigate the challenges and opportunities that come our way.

As we conclude this journey, I invite you to reflect on the insights and lessons you have gained along the way. Take some time to identify the areas where you have made the most progress, as well as the areas where you still have room for growth. Think about the actions and habits that have served you well, and those that you may need to adjust or improve.

Remember, success is not a destination, but a journey. It is a lifelong pursuit that requires constant learning, growth, and adaptation. But with the right mindset, skills, and support system, we can all achieve great things and leave a lasting legacy that we can be proud of.

I hope that the knowledge and insights you have gained through this journey will serve you well as you continue to pursue your own path towards success. Always remember that you have the power to create the life you want, and to make a positive impact on the world around you. Keep striving, keep learning, and never give up on your dreams.

Dear reader,

Thank you for taking the time to read this book. It means a lot to me that you chose to invest your time and energy into learning more about personal development and success.

I hope that you have found this book to be informative, insightful, and inspiring. My ultimate goal in writing this book was to provide you with practical tips and strategies that you can use to achieve your own personal and professional goals.

If you enjoyed this book and found it helpful, I would be grateful if you could leave a positive review on the platform where you purchased it. Your feedback can help others discover this book and benefit from its message.

Again, thank you for reading, and I wish you all the best on your journey towards success and personal growth.

Sincerely,

Anja

www.ingramcontent.com/pod-product-compliance
Lightning Source LLC
Chambersburg PA
CBHW070922220526
45467CB00004B/1508